GW01231015

The *Strands* series

1 *Nahda's Family*
2 *Pavan is a Sikh*
3 *Gypsy Family*
4 *Seven of Us*
5 *The Phoenix Bird Chinese Take-away*
6 *Islanders*
7 *A Farming Family from Wales*
8 *Shimon, Leah and Benjamin*
9 *Rebecca is a Cypriot*

British Library Cataloguing in Publication Data
Gwyndaf, Robin
  A Farming Family from Wales—(Strands' series; 7)
  1. Farm life – Wales, North – Juvenile literature
  2. Davies family – Juvenile literature
  I. Title   II. Finlay, Jeremy   III. Series
  942.9'1'08570922   S522.G7
  ISBN 0-7136-1919 8

A & C Black (Publishers) Limited
35 Bedford Row, London WC1R 4JH
ISBN 0 7136 1919 8

© Robin Gwyndaf 1979

All rights reserved. No part of this publication may be reproduced, stored in a retrieval system, or transmitted, in any form, or by any means, electronic, mechanical, photocopying, recording or otherwise, without prior permission of A & C Black (Publishers) Limited.

Filmset and printed in Great Britain by
BAS Printers Limited, Over Wallop, Hampshire

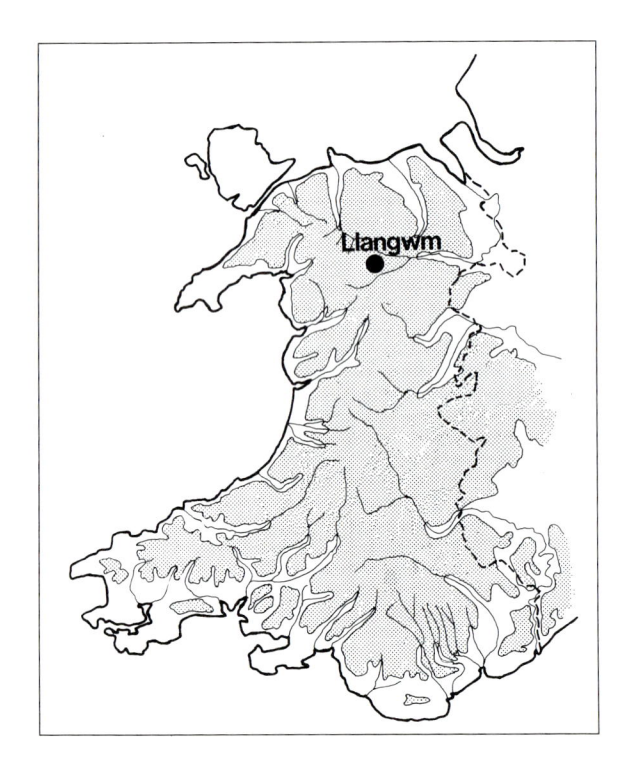

A Farming Family from Wales

Robin Gwyndaf
Photographs by Jeremy Finlay

Adam & Charles Black · London

Here is Nest and her grandmother. Nest is ten years old. Her grandmother (or Nain, as Nest calls her in Welsh) is eighty years old.

They are sitting in the parlour, where there is a Welsh dresser which was made over a hundred years ago by a local craftsman. On the shelves are blue willow-pattern plates. Nest sometimes helps her mother to dust the dresser, and she takes extra care not to break any of the plates! There is also a very old brass-faced grandfather clock. It is almost twice as tall as Nest.

Nest lives on a farm called Cefn Nannau, about a mile from the little village of Llangwm, in Clwyd, North Wales. It is not a very large farm, adding up to about 105 acres in all. There are eighteen fields, all with Welsh names, such as Cae Sgubor (the barn field), Cae Odisa Tŷ (the field below the house) and Cae Crwn (the round field). The names have been handed down from generation to generation.

In winter there is a lot of snow. Sometimes, instead of using a wooden sledge, Nest slides down one of the sloping fields inside a strong plastic sack, which her father once used to carry fertilizer.

Nest's surname is Davies, which is a fairly common name in Wales. Like most other families in the district, they always speak Welsh at home. Welsh is an old Celtic language. In fact, it is one of the oldest living languages in Europe.

Nest's family is a very close one. Here they all are having tea one Sunday afternoon. Although Nest likes cooking, she prefers going out and helping her father on the farm. She has one sister and one brother: Eirian who is eighteen years old and Iwan who is fourteen.

Eirian works in a bank at Corwen, about nine miles from Llangwm.

Nest's mother also goes out to work. She is a part-time district nurse and has a big black bag which she takes into the houses she visits. It is full of all the things a nurse needs.

Did you notice that Nain, Nest's grandmother, was not at the table having tea? She died in May, shortly after her picture in the parlour was taken. Nest and the family were very sad when she died. She was so gentle and kind. But Nest will always remember her happy face and all the interesting stories she used to tell.

On Nain's eightieth birthday, all her children and grandchildren came and gave her a big party. Now they are very glad they have a picture to remind them of that day.

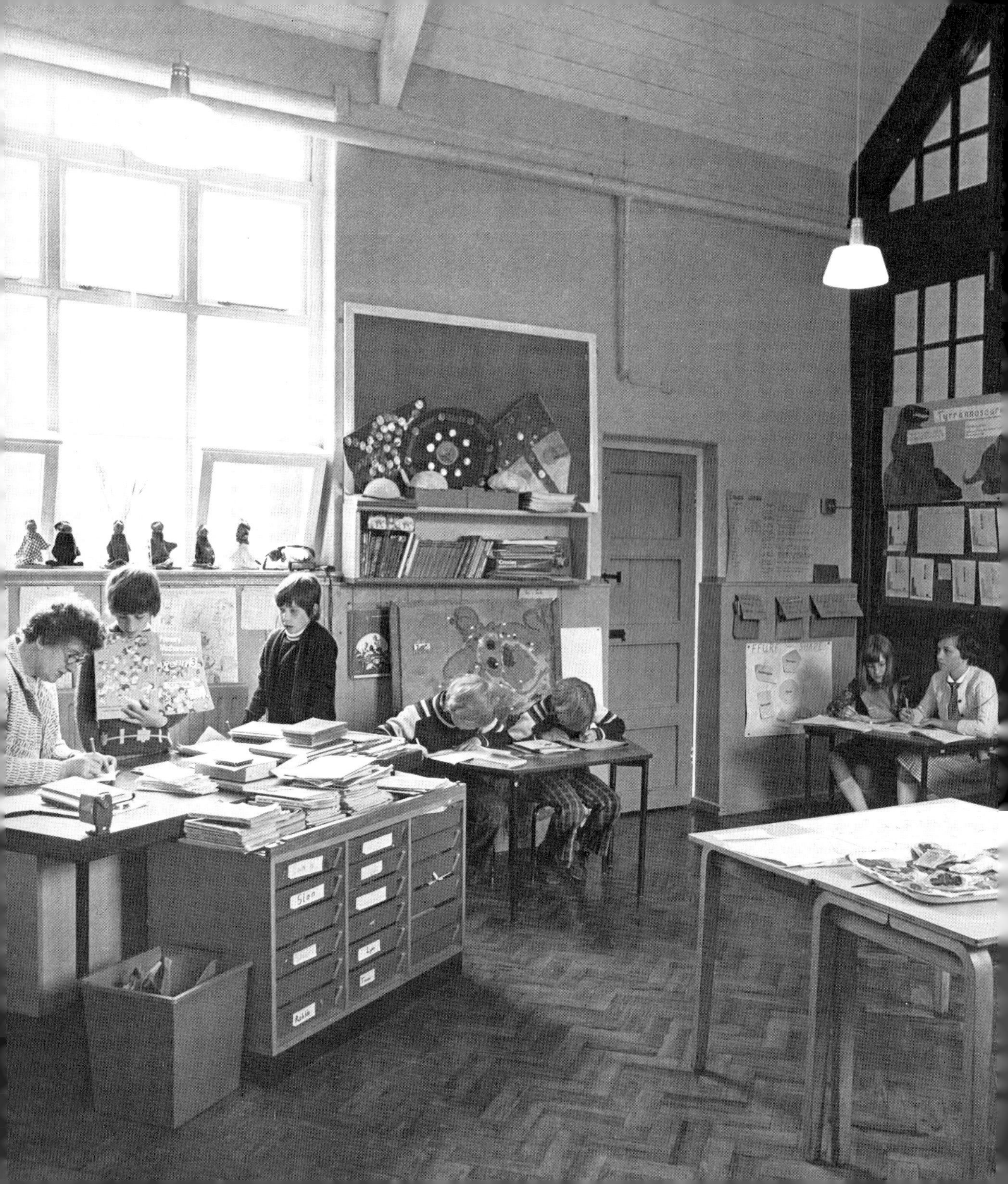
Tyrannosaur
Sion

Nest goes to the primary school at Llangwm. Her favourite subject is mathematics, but she also likes Welsh and English. It is a very small school, with only two teachers and twenty-five children. In September Nest will go to the comprehensive school at Llanrwst, over twenty miles away, and join Iwan her brother.

A brook runs past the school yard, and the children, especially the young ones, like to play on its banks. But in this photograph Nest sits on the bridge to show the photographer the coloured handbag she made herself. It won her equal first prize in a competition at the Llangwm eisteddfod.

Wales is a country well known for its eisteddfodau. Children and adults sing and recite in Welsh, and there are also competitions in literature and the arts and crafts.

Shortly before Christmas the Llangwm schoolchildren perform a nativity play. Last year Nest acted the part of Mary.

Nest and her family attend the Calvinistic Methodist chapel, which is only a few steps away from the farm.

Many of the congregation, especially the men, like to stand and talk outside the chapel before and after a service. There are three services on Sunday and also one or two meetings during the week.

Nest likes going to chapel, and especially to Sunday school. There are classes for all age groups.

The most important youth movement in Wales is Urdd Gobaith Cymru. Literally this means 'the league of the hope of Wales'. Every May the Urdd holds its own national eisteddfod in North and South Wales alternately. Winners from the district eisteddfod go forward to the county eisteddfod, and the winners there compete in the national.

Nest has competed only once in the national. It was held at Barry in Glamorganshire, and she was a member of the Llangwm recitation party.

In the ceremony of *cadeirio'r bardd* (chairing of the bard), the chair is awarded for the best poem written in a traditional and strict metre, called *cynghanedd*.

Local poets hold a big sword above the winning poet's head. Three times the host of the ceremony asks the question *A oes heddwch?* (Is there peace?). And the congregation replies three times *Heddwch*. The winning poet then sits in his chair. To end the ceremony the congregation sings the Welsh National Anthem.

The Llangwm eisteddfod is held in a marquee, in one of the fields near the village, during the last Saturday in June. In the preliminary tests of this year's eisteddfod, Nest competed in singing and reciting, but was not chosen to go on to the stage. She was, however, a member of the party that won the competition for singing *penillion* (verses) to the accompaniment of the harp.

Nest is very interested in local stories and traditions. Many years ago a cloud burst over the Foel Goch mountain, not far from her home. The water gushed down the hills and left deep scars in the ground which are still clearly visible today.

She is also interested in archaeology and old stones. There is one stone in the farm yard at Cefn Nannau which commemorates the work of a water diviner, called Robert Owen. He came to the farm in 1929 to look for water. He used a Y-shaped, freshly-cut hazel twig. The water diviner holds the twig firmly and horizontally in front of him with both hands while walking slowly across the land. Wherever there is a spring of fresh water the tip of the hazel twig bends towards his body.

Nest and Iwan had a pony once, but it was sold some time ago. They hope their father will soon be able to buy them another. One of Nest's best friends, who lives at the nearby farm of Ystrad Bach, has a pony called Dic. He is a strawberry roan and very beautiful. He has lots of character.

In September Nest fell off Dic and broke her arm, but it wasn't Dic's fault. Nest is still very fond of him and of all other animals.

She enjoys going with her father to the cattle market at Ruthin and to the sheep market at Denbigh. She thinks she might be a vet one day.

There are four dogs on the farm: Jess, Jeff, Ffan and Joc. Ffan doesn't like any kind of noise. When Nest and Iwan used to play cowboys and indians, or now when a cock crows, she barks and looks fierce. And you should see the cats run away in fright when Ffan or any of the other dogs come along! But they never bite. Whenever Ffan needs anything – especially food – she gets on her hind legs and taps on the kitchen window.

When Joc was a puppy he broke a leg. Nest's mother carefully placed the leg in a wooden splint, but Joc ate practically the whole splint and the bandage!

In August Iwan hopes to compete with Joc at the Llangwm sheep dog trials in the young shepherds' class. This means that he has to train hard with only three sheep. You certainly need a lot of patience and skill to be a good shepherd.

During March and April, when the lambs are born, Nest's father is very busy and both Nest and Iwan give him all the help they can. Recently, they had a pet lamb called Jill who was a very determined little thing!

When she grew up she simply would not go back to the fields and join the other lambs. When any of the dogs came near she would stamp one of her forelegs as if to say, 'Go away you dog!'

In March this year, when the weather was very cold, one sheep gave birth to three lambs. In case the mother hadn't got enough milk to feed them all, Nest gave them milk from a bottle. Now they have grown into strong lambs.

Another of Nest's tasks is to feed the young calves. This one is only three days old, and he is very difficult to control. Instead of drinking the milk he chews Nest's fingers, and when he finally puts his head in the bucket he scatters milk all over the place!

There are forty cows at Cefn Nannau. Iwan wants to be a farmer like his father, and he is already used to the job of milking the cows twice a day. He often takes his bike with him to bring the cattle in from the fields.

Until recently they had one, very old cow. She was big and tame, and Nest and Iwan used to ride on her back. She was a Guernsey, brown and white in colour, and gave rich, creamy milk. Nest and Iwan were sad when she had to be sold. But she left seven daughters, and two of them are still on the farm today. They are called Guernsey Glên (tame Guernsey) and Guernsey Wyllt (wild Guernsey). All the other cows are black and white Friesians.

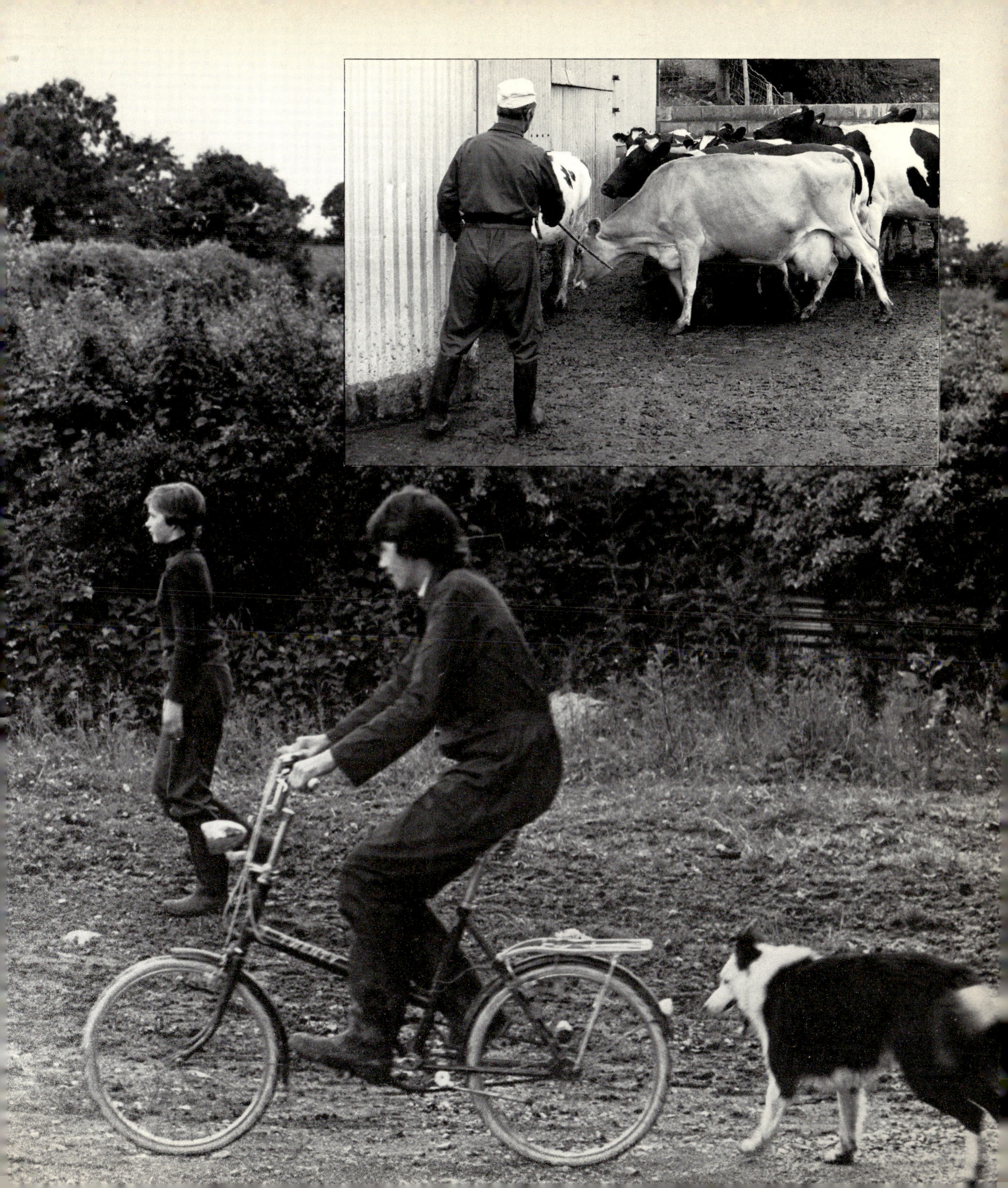

Nest and her father prepare the big tank which will hold the milk. The tank has to be kept very clean so that harmful germs won't infect the milk.

Until fairly recently milking was done by hand, but now it is all done by machine. At Cefn Nannau six cows at a time are brought from the shed into the milking parlour.

Each cow is given some 'cake' to eat, and its udders are carefully washed. The machine is placed on the cow's four teats and the milk is sucked into a pipe which takes it into the big tank. A lorry comes to the farm every morning to transport the milk to the factory.

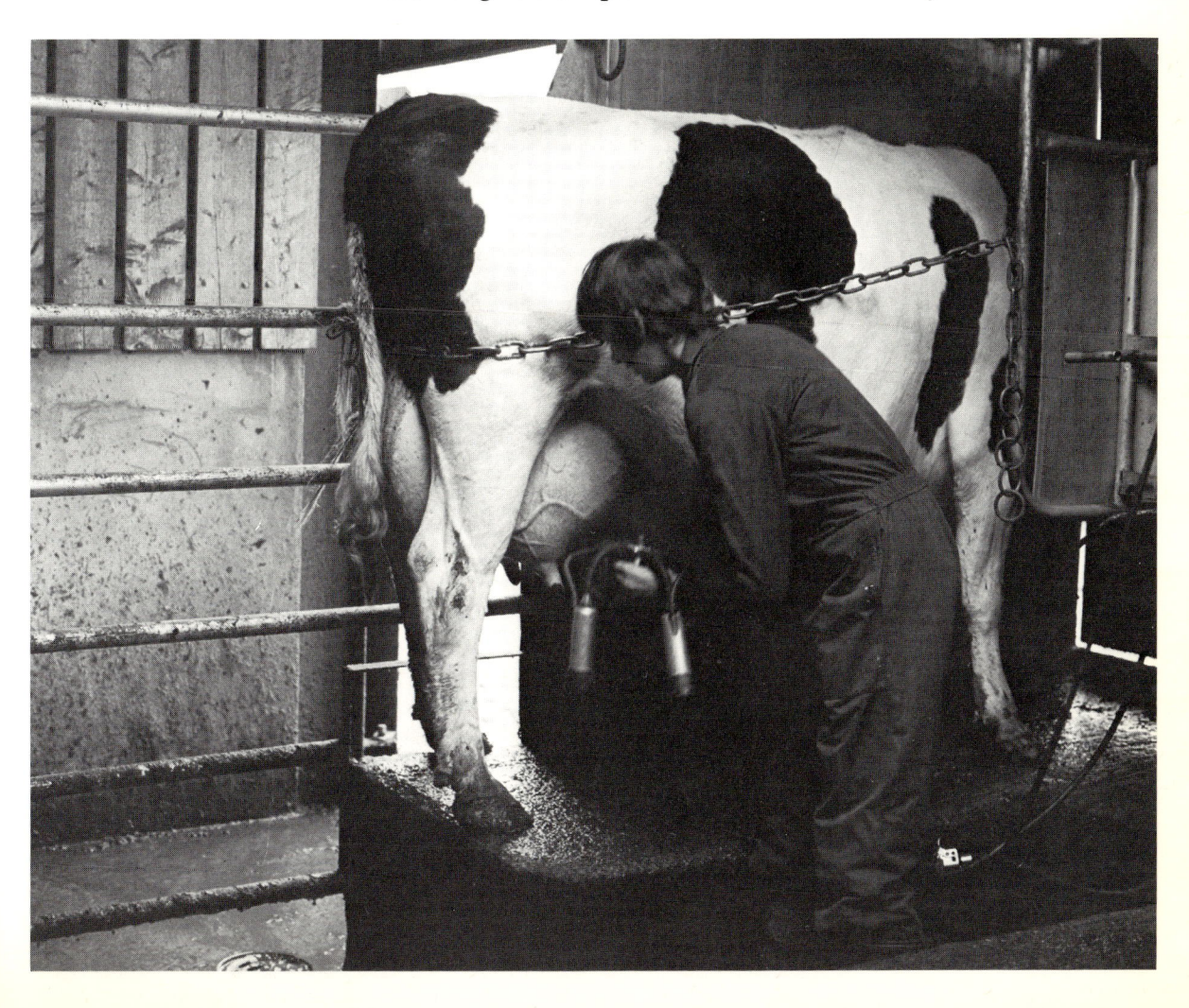

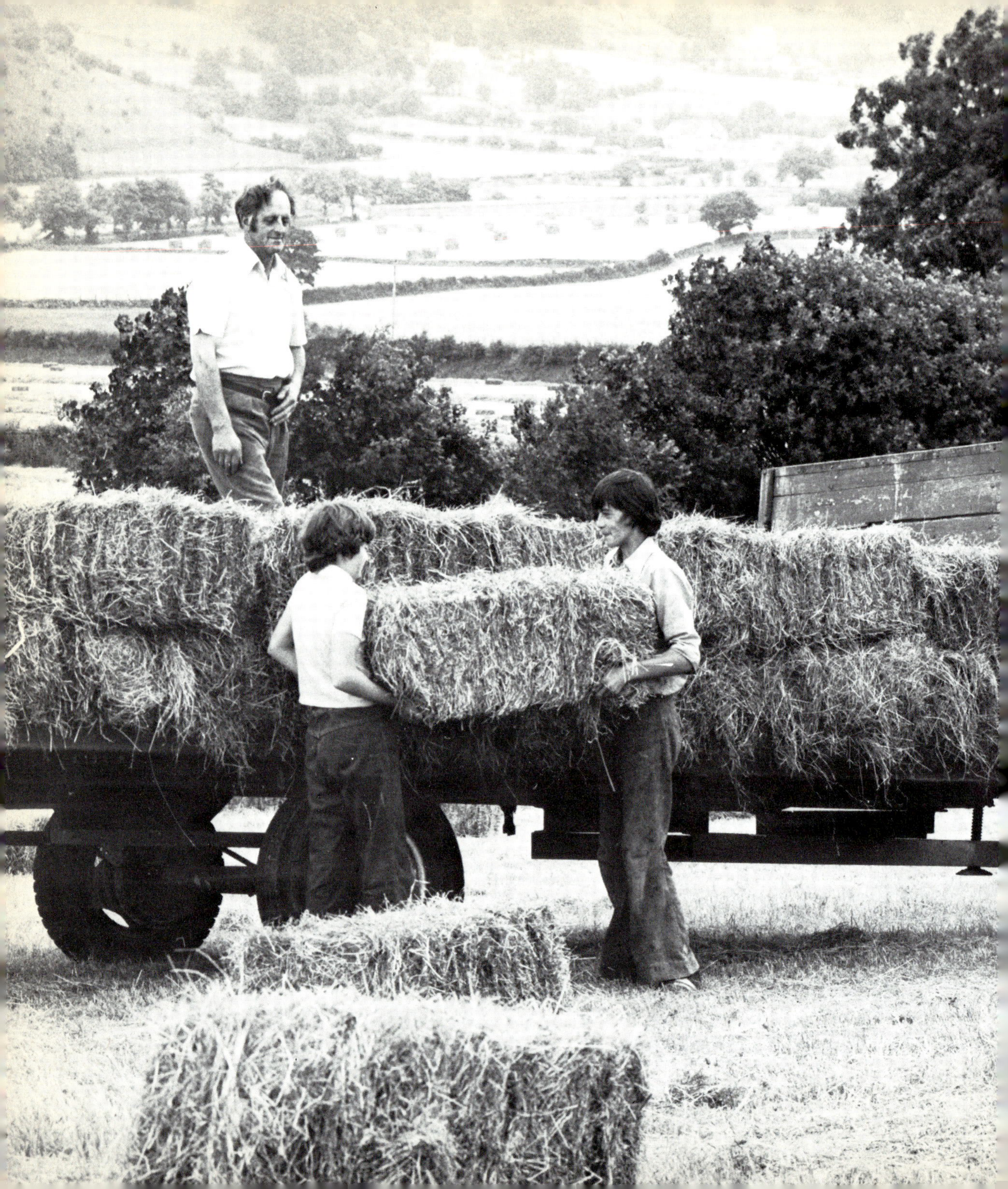

There are only a few hens at Cefn Nannau, but they lay lots of lovely brown eggs. During the day the hens' and chickens' favourite place is the barn, but towards the end of June they have to go somewhere else. This is the time for harvesting, and the barn will soon be full of tightly-packed bales of hay.

At harvest-time there is plenty of work for everyone. The bales are rather heavy for Nest to carry but, when work is finished, it's a wonderful feeling to sit on top of a load of hay as the tractor slowly rocks its way home.